Chalice of My Imagination

Chalice of My Imagination

Poetry & a Bit of Prose

Shirindokht Nourmanesh

Coyote Creek Books | San José | California

Printed in the United States of America

ISBN-13: 978-1-946647-07-8

25 24 23 22 21 20 19 18 17   1 2 3 4 5 6 7

Cover and illustrations by Shirindokht Nourmanesh
Front cover *The Poet, the Hermit*, watercolor on recycled paper
Back cover *Woman Tree,* acrylic on canvas

Author photo on back cover © Maral Mokhtari

Published by Coyote Creek Books
www.coyotecreekbooks.com

We seem normal, until we get together. That's when the sweet craziness of life starts, making it worth living.

I know you will face the world if it lays a finger on me.
I know you stand shoulder to shoulder with me when I need you.
I know you will never let me sink.
I know you never get old, and stay as annoying as you can be.
I know where you got your big hearts.
I know I am saner than you two.
I know you are the divine's gifts.
I know I am extremely blessed to have you as my siblings.

Behindokht …
Amirhossein …
You are the light of my eyes, and I love you.

Contents

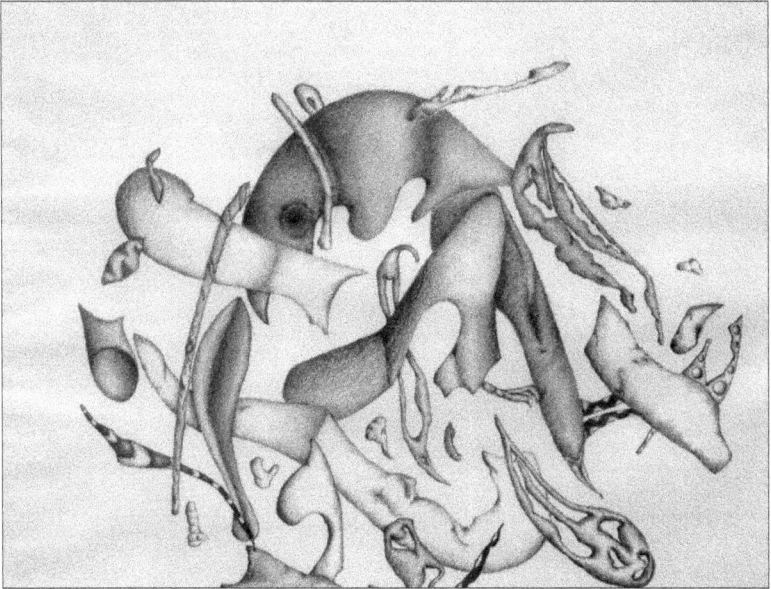

Twisted, pencil on sketching paper, 20" x 24"

SHAME

Tiny body parts sprinkled into the dust, images of souls buried under tons of cement, stones, iron rods, … bright orange body bags, each a human being, and tired fire fighters desperately holding back tears.

She rushes pass me toward her desk, her shoulder scratching roughly against my bare arm. In her hand, a rolled-up flag she pins to the board next to her son's picture. She looks at me in surprise.

"What's with you?" She asks.

"That atrocity" I choke.

"Yeah," she shrugs: "I know," and sighs a deep sigh.

I open my mouth to add something. "I know," she continues, "It is such a shame. Those were the second tallest in the world."

09/17/2001

زمانه ای دیگر بود

زمانه ای دیگر بود

آن گاه که

دستان من در پس کوچه های خودمانی خواستن

گل های شادمان بوسه را

به روی صورت باد

پرپر می کرد،

و

ایستاده روی سنگریزه های حوض لجن بسته

بوی ماندگی آب را

ـ مشت مشت ـ

به سوی آسمان می پراکند

*

لاجوردی کاشی ها

از سرخی لب های ماهی پُر بود

که قدم های سنگین باد

دانه های بنفش توت را لگد می کرد

و

قدم های کوچکِ من

به وسعت دلدادگی پدر

ـ به نسترن های باغچه خانه مان

جوانه داشت

*

پریدن از جؤیبار باریک

و نوشیدن از چشمه سنگ

یادگاری

... از روزگاری به غایت دور

... و

صدای جویدن دانه های انار

به زیر دندان های جوانی مادر

که در آن سوی جهان جای مانده است

در آن روزگاری که

با عینک گربه ای زرد

و شلوار کوتاهِ کاپری

چشمانش به رنگ سبزی پرنده های جنگل

و

صورتش پر از صورتی های پَرشکفته بود

... و لبخندش

ـ لبخندش

... به ملایمت آبی های دریا

A Different Time

A different time it was
—my small hands ripping happy kisses on the face of the wind
—my young bouncy feet running through familiar alleys of desire
—me standing on the algae-covered pebbles of the ponds
—me cupping the stillness of water up to the sky

The azure of the Persian tiles filled the red of fishes' lips
The wind's heavy strides trampled the purple of the mulberries
—my small steps filled with sprouts
as vast as my father's worship of the rose

Jump!
—me jumped over the tiny spring
Drink!
—me drank from the stones

Aw! How distant it seems.

Listen!
Here comes a noise—left on the other side of the world
—my young mother's chew on seeds of pomegranate
—my young mother a tiny little thing in yellow cat eye glasses and
60s Capri pants
—my mother's eyes as green as the feathers of the jungle

—my mother's face an ocean of blossomed pink

—her smile

—ah! her smile—

as soft as the blue of the sea

on this side

—me nailing the coffin.

A Different Time

Translated from English into the Hindi by Jhilmil Breckenridge

Ek alag vakht tha voh
—mere nanhe haath hawa ke chehre par chummiyan phenkte hue
—mere kudte hue pair jaani pehchaani chahton ki galliyon mein
daurte hue
—main talaabon ke kai se dhake hue patharon pe khadi
—main apne hathiyalon mein bhara pani aasman ko shradhanjali
karti hui
Phaaras ki nili taailen machliyon ke hoton ko laal bharti hain
Hawa ki bhaari kadmon ne shehtoot ka rang daba diya
—mere chote kadam ankurit se bhare
jaise mere pitaji gulabon ko pujte hue
Kudo!
—aur mai choti nadi ke upar se chalang koodi
Piyo!
—aur maine patharon se piya
Arre! Kitna door voh sab lagta hai.
Suno!
Ek aawaaz aai hai—duniya ke doosri taraf se
—meri ma bachpan mein anaar ke beej chaba rahi hain
—meri ma, 1960s ke kapree pant aur peele billiyon wale chashmon
mein, ek patli si cheez
—meri ma ki aankhen, junglon ke pankhon ki tarah hari

Chalice of My Imagination

—meri ma ka chehra gulaabon ka saagar

—unki muskuraahat

—hai, unki muskuraahat—

samundar ki neel ki tarah naazuk

Aur is taraf?

—kafan me kilon ki thonkne ki awaaz

A Different Time

Translated into French by Orang Gholikhani

C'était un autre temps

Ce temps où

Mes petites mains éparpillaient des baisers jubilatoires à la face du vent

Mes jeunes pieds bondissant couraient dans les rues familières de désire

Je me tenais debout sur les galets vaseux de la piscine

Je jetais—Poigné par poigné—l'eau stagnant au ciel

Le bleu azure des céramiques Persan remplissait la bouche des poissons rouges

Les pas lourds du vend piétinent les mûres pourpres

Et mes petits pas étaient plein de pousses

Aussi vaste que l'amour de mon père pour notre roserai

Saute !

Je sautais au-dessus de ruisseau

Bois !

Je buvais la source de pierre

Ah ! Comme il semble loin

Ecoute !

Chalice of My Imagination

Il arrive un bruit – laissé de l'autre côté du monde

Ma jeune mère mâchant les grains de grenade

Ma jeune mère une petite chose minuscule avec des lunettes de chat

jaunes et un pantacourt Capri

Les yeux de ma mère aussi verts que les plumes de la jungle

Le visage de ma mère un océan de bougeons roses

Son sourire

Ah ! Son sourire –

Aussi doux que le bleu du ciel

 De ce côté

Moi grattant un cercueil

Translated to Kurdish by Mohammad Assad Seraj-aldini

زەمانێکی تر

زەمانێکی تر بوو

ئەو کاتە

دەستەکانی من لە کۆڵانی ویست و خواستی خۆمالّی

چەپکە گولّی بزە و ماچی

ئەدا بەرووی شەمالّ و

پەڕ پەڕی نەکرد

راوەستا و لەسەر لێواری حەوزێکی لیخن

بەینی ناوی قەوزە گرتووی

مشت مشت

بە ئاسمانا ئەپژاند

شینی کاشیەکان

لە سووری ماسیەکان پڕ بوو

هەنگاوی بە هوژمی با

دەنکە توی سووری هەلّ نەوەراند

وە

هەنگاوی وردیلانەی من

بە پانای و ناخی خۆشەویستی باوکم

وەك خونچەی نەستەرەکانی باخچەکەمان

وەك چرۆ جوان

پەرینەوە لە جۆگەلەیەکی باریك

دەمی نایە ناو دەمی کانیاوی ژێر بەردێك

یادگارییەکە

لەو رۆژگارە هەرە دوورانە

مڵچەی چاوینی دەنکە هەنار

لە ژێر ددانی سەردەمی گەنجی دایکم

کە ئێستا لەوپەڕی دونیا بەجێ ماوە

نا لەو سەردەمەدا

بە عەینەکێکی دەور زەردی چاو پشیلە

وە پانتۆڵێکی کورتی (کاپری)

چاوەکانی رەنگی سەوزی باڵدارەکانی جەنگەڵی گرتبوو

ڕومەتی پڕ لە ناڵی گوڵی تازەکراوە

وە زەردەخەنەی

وە زەردەخەنەی

بەشینی و بڵاوینی ناوی دەریاکان

A Hole in My Heart

I feel a void today; a hole in my heart.
I don't love you anymore.
You think I'm lying?
Don't you love me no more?
[Na you don't.]

Life!
Ha; this ludicrous life.
It's now a gory habit—chains of bondage.
[Can't we just break away?]

On our way, twisted roads and hurdles,
Many dragons each with a thousand heads;
Conquered it all, confident.
Wasn't it love, a guide in our darkened nights?

Screw love.
It was love that fucked us in the first place.

Chalice of My Imagination

Simplicity of Break-up

Wake up, my darling
Wake up
      to the aroma of coffee
      and peace.

Listen to the silence
Listen to your heartbeat
      in the drums of your ears.

Taste the fresh air on your tongue
      when it swells
          –even to the memory of prosaic kisses
Taste your own bad breath.

Wash in the clean tub.
Leave the dirty dishes alone.

Have you noticed?
Have you noticed your heart
      right where you'd left it last?
Have you noticed the majesty of the morning
      in the absence of curse?

Turn on the radio to your favorite channel

Turn it on to your favorite scenario
Turn it on to your heart.

Listen to the noises of the neighbor's bedroom
Listen to the gasping of your mouth
       When it swells for a kiss
Listen
Listen to the making of love
       To the banging of heads
       To screech of the bed
       To the air—that is yours
       To the room and its walls
       To the pillow and your head
       that only wants the simplest things in life.

Listen to your sweet protagonist
Telling
       Telling your story.

Black Friday

Drip.
Drip.
Drip.
Soy latte.
Mocha—no cream—please.

Tick tock.
Middle aged.
Click.
Click.
Laptops in their faces
laptops on their laps
hopeful idiots, chanting:
We are going to write that
        great American novel.

The old woman with her
rolling walkers
talks about Harry
     —her idiot son.
     She had pulled all her money out
—she says, screeching her little wheels—
     and invested
     so today is a good day.

She is happy.

Clonk.
Clonk.
I listen to her dentures talk
about Harry;
Harry must have been a handsome man
        with a laptop stuck to his face.

Will he show up?
the man—my date—is not here yet.
He is late.
[They are always late.]

I hold on to the woman's walker. Tick tock.
I sit on the woman's chair. Tick tock.
I put my laptop in the woman's basket. Tick tock.
At least she has a son. Bravo.

Hopeful idiots
all are going to write
        that greatest American novel.
[Can you hear me Mr. Faulkner?]

I smell like mocha. No cream—I beg you.
The great American novel is a bitch:
"once a bitch, always a bitch."

and drips
loneliness and despair.

My dentures clonk
and I have no 401k.

Hmmm!
Something to contemplate on.

Chalice of My Imagination

You are the Chalice;
The chalice of my
Imagination.
The tip of your
Head drinking waves from
The river and
The fog finding its way
Through your knotted
Soul.

Combing
Brushing
Blowing the human out of me.

To borrow it from the Hawk
The Inhumane[1] in you
Scratches the particles of
breath out of me
And
Halleluiah
I am a Poet at last.

---

1 Reference to American poet Robinson Jeffers, his philosophy and his poetry

روز زرینِ شکفتن‌ها

چقدر این عکس‌های رنگی پرنور

که از باد

و هیاهوی زمان

خود را به دستِ قاب‌ها داده‌اند

زیبایند.

چقدر این چهره‌ها شادند.

چقدر من ...

در آن عکسی که سر بر شانه‌ات دارم

شادانم

جوانم

سرخوشم

خندانِ خندانم.

چقدر

تو ...

با بلوز آبی زنگالی نرم و لطیفت

و آن موی تُنُک بر لاله‌های گوش‌های بس‌ظریفت

ـ آرامی.

چقدر خوب است که ما این عکس‌ها را

به دستِ قاب‌های کاغذین و چوبی رنگین

سپردیم؛

چقدر خوب شد که ما این قاب‌ها را

به روی تاقچه‌های خاطره چیدیم.

چقدر خوب است که این قاب‌ها

و آن عکس‌های شاد و رنگ به رنگِ آفتاب‌خورده

من و ما را ...

در آن "های"

و

در آن "هوی" جوانی‌ها

از آن سوی پریدن‌ها

دویدن‌ها

رهایی‌ها

همیشه زنده می‌دارند.

چقدر یادآورانِ روزِ زرینِ شکفتن‌ها

مرا از آینه بیزار می‌سازند؛

دلم

ـ سخت ـ

از نگاهی بر برِ رخسارِ آینه،

می‌گیرد.

Golden Days of Rapture

How beautiful these photos are
sheltered in frames
from the commotion of the time.
How happy the faces.

How content I am
in that picture, my head on
your shoulder;
young
merry
jolly.
You in that soft cobalt blue
and your sparse hair over your delicate ears
you were gentle.

How wonderful we have entrusted our pictures
to cardboard frames
to wooden cases;
how fantastic
we aligned these casings
over the memory line.

How excellent these frames
and those sun-drenched colorful pictures

keep us alive
—you and I—
in the "hey"
and in the "ho" of youth
beyond the flight
        the flow
        the flee.

How the souvenir
of the golden days of rapture
make me hate the mirror;
my heart sinks
with every glance at the glass.

Doggie, X-ACTO knife on scraper board

Ha!

Parkway Expressway.
Uncivilized drivers.
Cradle of civilization.
Gray, nasty mucus
      Out of my nostrils;
This is my beloved city, Tehran[2]!
Honk! Honk!

Nauseated—I am—out of
My brain cells.
Punished by migraine.
Honk! Honk!

This is my childhood
Gushed out of my mouth
      All over a Mercedes.
BEAUTIFUL!!
Honk! Honk!

Color of blood,
      Red lips
      Red eyes
Ecstasy! Vodka!

---

2 Capital of Iran

Shirindokht Nourmanesh

Honk loud if you want me.

Honk if you want to lick the red running down my thighs.

Honk! Honk if you want to throw me a stone.

Honk! Honk!

Black

Black chador

Black heart of the sky

Dark, nasty mucus of crude oil

Raining down on me.

Honk if you want oil.

Honk! Honk!

In this bigger than biggest red-light district

Throw me a stone

If you want oil.

Throw me a stone

If you want sex.

Throw me a stone

If you are zealous

If you're concerned.

Pick the biggest.

Honk! Honk!

Ha!

Translated into Turkish by C.S. Kayatekin.

Parkway yolu:
Sürücüler, medeniyetsizler,
Medeniyetin beşiğindekiler.
Bu sümük – gri ve pis
      Damlar, damlar burnumdan.
Bu benim - benim şehrim, benim aşkım, benim Tehran'ım.
Biip! Daat!

Miğdem bulanık – kalmadı artık
Beynimde boşluk.
Of, bir baş ağrısı!
Daat! Daat!

Bu benim çocukluğum
Ağzımdan akan,
      Mersedes'i boyayan.
Ne güzellik!
Biip! Biip!

Kan renginde
Kırmızı dudaklar,
Kırmızı gözler.
Coşku! Vodka!

Öttür o kornayı, iştahın benim içinse;
Öttür o kornayı, gözünü çektiyse bacağımdan damlayan o kırmızı,
Öttür o kornayı, elindeki taşı atmak ise isteğin
Daat! Daat!

Siyah;
Siyah burkalı;
Siyah yürekli gökyüzü.
Petrol - koyu, pis sümük gibi
        Yağar başımıza.
Öttür o kornayı, iştahin petrol ise.
Daat! Daat!

Burada, bu mahallede, kırmızıfener muhitinde,
At bir taş, bu yöne.
İştahın petrol ise,
At bir taş, benim önüme;
Sulanman seksim içinse,
At bir taş, ayaklarımın dibine;
At bir taş, ey köpüren!
At bir taş, ey endişelenen!
At, hele en büyüğünden.
Daat! Daat!

Ha!

Translated into the Hindi by Jhilmil Breckenridge

Parkway ki Express Highway

Jahaan drivers insaan nahi, haiwan hain

Insaaniyat ke palne mein

Salaiti, ghinoni kaf

Meri nathna se tapakti hai

Yeh mera parampriya sheher, Teheran, hai

Pain! Pain!

Matli — Aur mere dimaag

Ke cell khatam

Behad sirdard

Pain! Pain!

Yeh mera bachpan hai

Jo mere mooh se nikla

Ek Mercedes Par

Ati sundar!

Pain! Pain!

Khoon ka rang

Laal hont

Laal aankhen

Ekstacy! Sharaab!

Agar mujhe chaahte ho, to zor se horn bajao

Agar meri jaangho se tapakta laal chaatna chahte ho, horn bajao

Agar meri taraf pathar phenkna chahte ho, horn bajao

Pain! Pain!

Kaala

Kaali chaadar

Kaala dil aasman ka

Kaali, andheri, kacche tel ki kichad

Mere upar tapak rahi hai

Agar tel chahiye, horn bajao

Pain! Pain!

Is sabse bade vaishyon ke mohalle mein

Mere upar pathar phekho

Agar tumhe tel chahiye

Mere upar pathar phekho

Agar tumhe sex chahiye

Mere upar pathar phekho

Agar tum mazhabi ho

Agar tum utsaahi ho

Sabse bara pathar chunnana

Pain! Pain!

Chalice of My Imagination

Heavenly Blessings

Stupid Dido
Why did you have to
leave me alone?
He was only after his
own crown.

There is no way back from
Hades, and the Heavens are
          not crying for you;
It's just Poseidon
Pissing on us.

ستایش

در گیرودارِ آتشِ تن
دستانِ پُرشرارتِ توست
که به انگیزه‌ی رهاسازی‌ام زِ خویش
خاموشيِ خروشِ غریزه را داد می‌زند.

چون است
که در تلاطمِ خوش‌نسیمِ آمیختن
زیبایی هجومِ هوس‌های سرخوشی،
انگیزه‌ی ستایشِ خویشتن می‌شود.

Turbulence of Coupling

In the throes of body heat
your mischievous hands
utter the death of instinct
to free me from myself.

Hence,
the praise of I
after the beautiful influx of intoxicated lust
      in the welcoming turbulence of coupling.

سِترورن

آیا می‌توان مرا به باد سپرد؟
آیا ...
من از جنس گرگ‌دههای گل نیستم
که سنگینی پیکرم
دست‌خوش شناوری توفان‌هاست؟

بر باد می‌نشینم
که از تکرارها روم.
سرخوش
– چو گرگ‌ده‌ی سبکِ بی‌نهایتی –
بر بالِ باد
به همه‌جا می‌روم.
سودی نبرده‌ام
از این یک‌مکان‌شدن؛
با دستِ باد
به هَرجا می‌روم.

شاید

گلِ خسته‌ی بیمار بی‌هوس

با من بیامیزد از فرطِ ناخوشی:

بارورها شود؛

بارورها شوم.

The Infertile

Translated into English by Dr. Persis Karim

Is it possible to give me to the wind?
Am I not a flower?
The lightness of its pollen
Scattered by storms?

I sit on the wind delighted
To escape this repetition.
Like a boundless, light seed
On the wings of the wind
I go everywhere.

I haven't gained anything
Remaining in one place.
In the hands of the wind
I go everywhere.

Perhaps
I will find another
Tired flower, whose ache
And mine will join
And make our communion
Pregnant with possibilities.

Paisley Dream, pencil on drawing paper, 22" x 30"

میگرن

به یاخته‌های صبوری‌کشیده‌ام چه بگویم؟

که درد شرمسارم کرده است.

دیگر حتی دیوار سنگی هم

درمانِ جمجمه‌ی درد نیست.

بسیار نیاز دست‌انداختن به این چَشم را دارم.

حدقه‌ی بینایی من

همانا که چون آتشفشانی از خون و لنف و عصب

به سقف تارِ اتاق بپاشد.

این سر پُربار پُرهوا

پنهان،

درون این دو دستِ باریکِ بی‌هنر،

بی‌هوده مانده است؛

طفیلیِ همیشه‌بیمار را

چاره‌ای جز تبرزین نیست.

Migraine Headache

What can I say
to my patient throbbing brain cells?
I am ashamed of all
the torture.
Not even the stone wall
is the remedy to the skull of
pain.

I need to claw
this eye.
This ball is
to explode any minute
up to the dark ceiling
in a grotesque bursting
of blood
of nerve
of lymph.

This head,
this grave solemn head,
left in vain
—hidden—
within these good-for-nothing
hands.

One cure for the parasite:
the axe.

Shush …

There was not enough room
For him
And I
And his midlife crisis
In his Z4 Roadster;
Thus, I asked him to leave.

I was afraid
He would strangle me
With the thick gold band on his wrist;
So, I asked him to leave.

I couldn't sleep,
I told him.
It's just me, you know;
I asked him to leave.

He hugged the pillow
With his good hands
Hid his face in it;
Are you a prostitute? he asked.

I asked him to leave;
And

I forgot to ask for his name.

Now I am sitting here,
With his pillow on my lap
Not remembering my name.

Was I crucified,
or did I burn on stake?
Was it me who passed the Tigris
bundled in Ishtar's blanket?
Was it me whose name kept
hidden in Hammurabi's code of laws?

Should I dial another number?

My Mythos

My beauty is my
Force of imagination
Seeds of pomegranate
Crushed
Within the pumping of my
Heart
And at the beginning there was
Word
A saint on cross
And I drop from
Rain
Nothing …
Nothing as wise as I
And in my mythos
I bear resemblance to Zeus
Making you dwarfed
In my presence.

Ode to Pen

bleed
bleed my beloved
bleed the ink of conscience
          through the pores of your mind's eye
let it run
amongst the cells of your fiber

bleed

do not cry
you did not play a role
          in my execution
it was the Pen
forcing out my imagination
onto the whiteness of
          your surface
making love
to the immensity of
you
and I
just a witness
alas
the love triangle between us
cannot feed me

during this hunger strike
in the corner of my cell

I am indebted to her
for my doomed fate
and I love you for your patience
during all that rubbing
of her flesh

you and I all we need
is her
and what torture
can be worse than now
they deny us
her touch

the three of us
could have an orgy tonight
now that I am in pain
and now that I foam from mouth
and my bruised body
burns in fever
and I have fresh flesh for my nails
my hallucination
is what feeds my Temptress
in her highest state of inkling
we could have created

Chalice of My Imagination

a masterpiece
tonight

they don't let me be
even now
that I am
walking to the lynching tree
and this tree
reminds me of you
and of her
and the touch of her mouth
on the whiteness of
you

do not cry for me
you did not play a role
         in my execution

tell every one
         not to forget me
even if they say
I was nobody
just a person
who
writ

Offerings

Last time I offered you
an apple,
there was a blessing in it;
I saved your sorry buttocks
from a boring life.

Now, under my fingertips
the white marble of your chest,
crushes your claustro—
            phobic heart
taking you to the dominion of the Wise
and, you still blame me for
your circumcised head.

It's not that I believed in you;
It was in my nature to
share,
and I knew
you were green to your teeth
to let me have something of my
own.

You keep pushing back my extended hand
and I am trying to let you see

I am not your typical—
Silence;
I've been told not to give up my seat
anymore.

Keep on refusing.
Next time I eat it
myself.

Offerings

Translated into Swedish by Rana Rezapour

Sist jag erbjöd dig ett äpple,

Fanns det en välsignelse inuti det,

Jag räddade ditt sorgsna skinn från ett tråkigt liv.

Nu under mina fingertoppar

Den vita marmorn från din byst,

krossar ditt klaustrofobiska hjärta -

tar dig till de klokas herravälde

dock, klandrar du mig för ditt omskurna huvud.

Det är Inte att jag trodde på dig;

Det fanns i mitt naturliga innersta att dela

och jag visste att du var för avundsjuk för att Låta mig ha något eget.

du fortsätter att avvisa min utsträckta hand och jag försöker få dig att

inse att jag är ingen vanlig människa.

Tystnad;

Jag har fått rådet att inte längre avstå från min plats.

Fortsätt att vägra

Nästa gång förtär jag det själv.

Chalice of My Imagination

Midwinter Revolt, acrylic on canvas

Once a lover

And then the silence was unbearable.

Nothing left of my voice
I screamed inside
and the silence
so loud
I couldn't hear the tear drops in my throat.

The silenced I
in the middle of the room
hush puppies on the table
and I a dog of quiet means
hushed on the floor
hands and fists
whispering love on my eyes
and my ribs
quietly breaking
quietly healing.

Let us not break the silence.

But where your soul has gone, I asked myself,
quietly,
you were once a lover.

Cold shoulder and I knew the wall was too high
silently reaching for the sky.

Reflection!

You!
Hey you!

Your eyes.
Your distant eyes.
Frosty;
      Frosty cold.

You!
Your eyes
Burn every fiber of my being
While the nothingness of me
Cuts me
in the heart
Slaps me
in the face.

And
There you are
With those eyes
      Those frosty cold eyes
Their white red with rage,
Gazing
Gazing

Gazing at me
Questioning my most intimate thoughts
And
Your eyes
Tell me I am the
      enemy.

Disappointed?
Disappointed you are,
      I know!

Have I failed?

If only I could break this glass.

The Scarlet Letter

O' Father!

You can't bear the shame
You slash your throat
You can't stand the disgrace
You slash my throat

I end up in a well
While your throat heals
And your voice
      —irritated with broken honor—
Recites verses of the holy and the devout.

You have taken away my pearl
And I have become a stranger
to you
O' Father
O' Heavenly Father.

From Seneca to Badakhsh
I lean on the moon to stand
And for hundreds of years
I burn on cross
While I dance to the four-four beat of Disco music

O' Father
O' Heavenly Father

I stand tall at the bottom of the well
With my scarlet letter
on my chest.

Forgive me Father
I have sinned.

Forget me Father
I am gone.

Chalice of My Imagination

Much Obliged

No need to get out of bed;
I didn't come
          to stay.

Will be gone
after a puff.
I'm much obliged;
you must be
          tired.

نه!
از تخت بیرون نیا.

نیامده بودم که بمانم.

پس از این سیگار خواهم رفت.

زحمت کشیدی.
شرمنده.

به همین سادگی

ساده ساده ساده

عاشق که می‌شوم

مغشوشم و گیج و، یک‌هو،

لکه‌دار.

گاهی سقوط می‌کنم از

صخره تا هبوط

گاه سرم به سنگ،

نتیجه‌ی بدخیم هرزگی.

گاهی دلم غیژ

گاه قیقاج می‌رود

بالا

سقوط

بعد جرنگ شکستن است و بس.

خار می‌شوم،

تیغ،

و یک دفعه گُل از گُلم بُروز.

دست‌دست می‌کنم.

معشوق که می‌شوم،

بی‌تابِ بلاغت جسم،

هِن‌هِن و یک ملافه عرق

نفس به نفس

و یک اتاق ستاره و شهاب.

دل می‌بندم

و آن،

گاهِ رفتن است.

ساده ساده ساده

عاشق که می‌شوم

من لکاته

و همه اثیرِ بوفِ کور.

As Simple as That

It is very simple.
When I fall in love
I become astray and confused
–and suddenly–
stained.

Sometimes I plunge from
a cliff to a pimp
now and then, my head
to a rock
malignant results of promiscuity.
My heart soars
high
low
then comes the shattering tinkle,
and nothing more.
A thorn I become,
a spike
a cactus, flowered.

I procrastinate.

When I become a lover,

enamored I

—impatient of the rhetoric of the flesh—

pants under sheets of sweat

breathe to breathe

and a room full of meteors

and suddenly,

it is time to leave.

It is very simple.

When I fall in love,

I am the harlot

Others,

blind owls—ethereal women.

As Simple as That

Translated into French by Orang Gholikhani

C'est aussi simple que ça
Quand je tombe amoureuse
Je suis confuse et étourdie et
—D'un coup—
Entachée

Parfois je chute
Du rocher jusqu'au bas fond

Tantôt je prends une pierre sur le visage
Conséquence dramatique de la débauche

Parfois mon cœur s'emballe
Tantôt il déraille

En haut
La chut
Puis tintement de la cassure et rien d'autre

Je deviens épine
Une pointe
Et tout d'un coup, une fleur de cactus

Chalice of My Imagination

Je temporise

Quand je deviens une maitresse amoureuse
—impatiente de l'éloquence de chair—
Nue sous un drap de sueur
Souffle contre souffle
Et une chambre plein d'étoiles filantes
Mon cœur s'attache
Et soudain
C'est le temps de partir

C'est aussi simple que ça
Quand je tombe amoureuse
Je suis la catin
Et les autres, les hiboux aveugles—les femmes éthérées

Start with …

Start with,
Hi, good to see you again.
Recognize me.
Hi, it's nice to see you too.

Ask me how I have been.
Ask me how my day has gone.
I would like that.
Ask me how life has been treating me.
I would love that.
Ask me if I want to see the sunset.
Ask me about my favorite color,
      my favorite flower,
      my favorite song.

Remember, and remember me.

Remember the color of my eyes.
Remember what I wore the first time we met.
Remember to ask me how I feel.
Remember to start with a call.
Start with a call.
Start with hi.
I will answer; I make sure to answer.

I will start with you if you call.

I will start with you
        All over again.

Warning!

Asymmetrical she, twisted that woman
Unpredictable tornadoes
      Inside
Bright and sunny, her exterior just to fool the world.
She knows how to hide
      the woman with a thousand tongues,
      the woman with layers of skin.

She can be as sweet as her name implies.
She has the sweetest smile you have seen
The friendliest eyes
      hazel with a tint of green and yellow
The warmest hello
      soft and blue.

She uses lots and lots of red, and orange, and yellow
In her paintings.
Her heart–red, and the arrow she shoots
      to the sky is of
      flesh and of lots of blood.

I shall not stand in her way
I know she will not hesitate to point the arrow at me.

I shall not mess with her
I know she can make me very irregular.

And I am sure, someday,
She will publish this.

Boy Interrupted, ink on paper

Water and Dirt

Your footsteps on my heart
slush of the youth
risen from the impure dirt of juvenile need.

I asked you not to mud the water
        it feeds the plains down the river
alas you didn't listen.

The first woman had risen from
water
your tainted hands
confined her into dirt.

This Dull Pain

I thought I would change the world.
Ha Ha Ha!
Funny, how it changed me that old whizzing—I want to say—
witch—and I know
It's not politically correct.

Now my eyes miss something;
something that speeds away my voiceless-ness
—is this even a word?
Darting rush of ink
to blow away this dull dull dull
pain
of this shield I hide behind.

From one room to the other,
her smile floats like an angel with golden wings
—I am dreaming again.
I have followed her departure
and nothing
absolutely nothing
but walls of despair rose in front of me.

Chalice of My Imagination

Just Another Headache

I want to say it's just another headache.

Sharp pain
Blurry vision
Nausea.

My face in the toilet bowl
Pieces of chicken in water
Ice pad at the top of my head.
I pull my hair.

I want to say it's just another headache.

That noise
That banging in my head
Behind my eye balls.

Is the room turning?
Should I bang my head to the wall?
Should I smash it into pieces?

I want to say it's just another headache.

Nausea.

Eye balls.
Pain. Pain. Pain.

Let me introduce you to my nemesis.

Ladies and gentlemen,
Here is migraine.

You'd Think, I Painted It Myself

Hanging from the curtains, its end hops over the wooden table like the uneasiness of my fluttering heart. It crawls, hurried, from the wall to the door. Comes luminous, rushed, as if nothing is left of this life. As if looking for a missing lover; my heart, clawing my chest. You'd think it'd flood out of my mouth over the half-burnt Persian. Veiling half of the carpet in red in yellow, and it leaps. My back to the wall, with no gap to let me go, facing a blazing wall.

I told him to put out the fire. I told him to be cautious of the sparks. I did, he said, I put it out. What happened? Where is he? I call him and my voice fades away in the screech and the creak.

I am left facing a blazing wall and a dark smoke burning my throat. What a spat. Bounces with the fervor of a dancer, crawls swift and fast, it burns; its burning you'd think the sun setting on a cloth canvas.

I told him to put out the fire. I did, he said. Where is he now? Faster than this fire, he came, hopped, and left. I call him and my voice silenced in the yellow in the red does not return.

Galaxy of sparks; bright, blinking, thousands of little suns. Fast, enamored, bewildered. Rupturing the wood under its teeth. Groaning of the wood, and my back to the wall. How scorching, how fast the Persian burns toward me in red in yellow in orange. As if a painter's brush spreading blue and red forward, orange and a meager green in return. Moves forward again in red in yellow, crawls back in orange.

I told him to put out the fire. I did, he said.

Smell of smoke, and my throat burns. Smell of burnt flesh, as if branding me with a hot iron rod. What a beauty this red, this yellow and orange, how fast they interweave, like the orange I spread over the sun, the red that dripped from the tip of my brush over the floor, heaving his shout. You would think I painted this scene myself. How fantastic. What a scorching heat, hurried and restless. Crawls underneath my feet, attacking me in the face. On my toes. One foot. Both feet. Hopscotch. One foot, both feet. Hot. Toes. Heels. A scream. Moaning, and the smell of burning flesh suffocating me. The hot peels my skin. Burns. What a bad smell. It's worse than the time he burned my skin with steam.

You'd think I've painted it myself. I told him to put it out. I did, he said.

You'd think it's me burning. As if this is my own burnt hair pasted to my skin. Fried I. Roasted fat mixed with synthetic cloth.

A long cable flogging the gorgeous flames as if punishing a dancer for the boogie.

You'd think I've painted it myself. I told him to put it out. I did, he said.

Someone's shrieking. I feel my eyeballs have melted. There comes a siren. Here comes the ceiling. I should have left before my scorched heart got sprinkled out of my blistered chest on this burnt carpet.

I told him to put it out. Don't worry, he said, I will put you out.

The Magnificent You

An splendor poplar tree,
      You are the home to love.
Morning breeze on yellow tulips and a romantic ballad,
      You are the singing lexicon of a love affair.
A cry of silence, and
      the endless moaning of a wave,
Yet the end of nonexistence,
And the conclusion of all the far-away silent roads;
You are lovely.

An embracing branch of dawn,
You are the glory of the season of rain and roar of rivers.

Pure
Fruitful, and
      Passionate,
You are the fanfare of calm beatings of my heart.

A meadow of raindrops, and
      A cloudless Spring coppice,
You are the freshness from within the roots of the earth,
The air in its lungs.

You are the Arash's arrow piercing my heart,

A vine embracing it.

You!
The everlasting you,
The vigilante beauty—You,
You are prayers of the dawn
        Verses of holy books
        A house of worship
You, an unmatched Persian cat
A lonely lion.

You are silent—
Proud
Darling.
You are the chalice of love;
You are *The Love*.
You are Home.
Glory of my faith,
You are my motherland.
The origin of me.
The end of me.
Me.

And I Become the Cycle

The oak tree, beautiful
Elegant
Dry
Not that many leaves left of her youth
I asked if I could talk to her
A branch shuttered
And she—crossing her arms—refused.
I asked again, and walked away thanking her
—that sad, beautiful tree.

The earth moved within me
With each step I took
The earth
Connected to me
Through the soles of my shoes
I should have taken off my shoes, I thought;
Why was I hesitant to take off my shoes?

The raven
Magnificent
Loud
Black
Naughty
Called me to himself

I walked toward him in steady steps
With a heart longing for love
Earth moving through my soles
Through my body.

I asked if I could talk to him
He started walking, and I followed in steady steps
Earth going through me
Moving in me
Around me
Pulling me into her womb
The raven witnessing the Union,
And I still had my shoes on.

I followed the magnificent bird
In love with his voice
With his song
Loud
Strong
Solitary.

He flew over and sat on a tree, I followed
Mesmerized by his voice
His black
His feathers

I followed and stood underneath

He dropped a leaf.
I hold the leaf in my palm
I followed him again from
One tree to the next
Earth moving inside me
Around me
And I walked around the tree
The raven watching me with patience

He asked me to look at the
Dead leaves
At the dry brownish
Dead leaves
Covering the grass around the tree.

He asked me to see
To open my eyes, and see
The new green
The new leaves
Peeking out
From within the dry
Brownish
Pile of leaves.

Life continues, he said,
and the cycle goes back

Shirindokht Nourmanesh

to the beginning
and repeats itself over again.

I agreed,
So, he asked me to remember
Go tell the first tree, he demanded,
Go remind her she will flourish again.

The tree smiled when I told her
And let me back on my way
With the raven's gift in my heart
And the earth running through me.

I walked away with shoes in hand.

Chalice of My Imagination

Buzzing of Words

Last time I woke up
A vulture was feeding on my flesh,
And an owl was contemplating on the relationship between
My body to myself, to the vulture, vulture to the earth, earth to the
moon,
Moon to the howls of a wolf.

Last time I slept
The moon was orange and the sun was hiding behind the agonies of
interrupted lives
Of refugees
Of death on the shores of Lesbos.

Tonight, I walked in the rain
In San Francisco
—Where many have left their hearts—
With a man who reeked curry
And loved seeing himself with a golden crown,
And I didn't have the heart to tell him his chakra was washed in rain.

I had never walked around town in rain
—In my night gown, and
Barefoot—
But when I am naked,

The whole city dwells in me.

You have stumbled upon a body that never rests
A brain with its hissing bees
—Yellow and black—
And a queen—manicured and huge—
Sitting on eggs full of words.

You may drink me whenever you want.
You may taste me in your arms.
I am from the lineage of the lexicon queens,
And come from where rain turns into sand
Where poets rot in prison cells
And fly with one broken wing.

Chalice of My Imagination

Translators

Jhilmil Breckenridge is a poet, writer and activist. She is passionate about issues of women, disability, and mental health. Jhilmil is currently working on a PhD in Creative Writing from the University of Central Lancashire in the UK. She is Fiction Editor for South Asian leading literary journal, *Open Road Review* (openroadreview.com) and is editor for thewomaninc.com, an initiative highlighting women's issues of abuse and domestic violence. She has recently founded a charity in India, Bhor Foundation (bhorfoundation.wordpress.com) and one of their initiatives is to take poetry as therapy into asylums and prisons.

A native of Tehran, **Orang Gholikhani** arrived in Paris in 1979. He carried with him a pack of Iran's soil which later was spread out throughout the Parisian pavement. While he studied computer Science and has worked with large corporations, he managed to write poems in Persian and French, which reflect French images with a Persian fragrance. Orang's first collection of poems in Persian, titled *The Fourth Season*, was published in 2012 by H & S Media: www.handsmedia.com/books/?book=the-fourth-season, and his second book, THE SEASON OF INFINITE LINES, a bilingual Franco-Persian collection of poems, was published in 2015 at https://tinyurl.com/l7kghjb.

Persis Karim is a professor in the Department of English & Comparative Literature at San Jose State University where she teaches ethnic American Literature, World Literature and Middle East Studies. She is the founding director of the Persian Studies program, and the author of numerous articles about Iranian diaspora literature and culture. She is the editor of three anthologies of Iranian-American literature and a poet. Her work has appeared in numerous literary journals including *Callaloo, Reed Magazine,*

Caesura, HeartLodge and numerous others. You can learn more about her at her website: www.persiskarim.com.

C.S. Kayatekin is a designer and academic whose research is focused on the topic of urban resilience and inclusivity, with a specific interest in the clash of the local and the global within the affairs of cities worldwide. He was born in Ankara, Turkey, and currently maintains one foot in the United States, wherein he is finishing his doctoral studies, and one foot in Sri Lanka, with his wife, a Kandyan architect. His connection to Shirindokht Nourmanesh can be traced back to his continued collaboration with Sepa Sama, an artist now based in Sweden firmly engaged in the subject of diaspora and cross-cultural identity, among other topics.

Rana Rezapour was born and raised in Iran, then moved to Sweden at the age of 18. After obtaining a degree in Civil Engineering from the Royal Institute of Technology in late 1999, she moved to Canada, and in December of 2011 to California. In 2015, she lived in Morocco for ten months, and while there, started designing bags and now has her own small business. Rana has always done humanitarian and volunteer work; has worked at orphanages while in Morocco, traveled to Honduras and Ghana with IVHQ and Global Brigades, making toilets for children's schools, renovating clinics, and helping the less fortunate to have medicine and dental care. She has also been involved with Habitat for Humanity, American Red Cross, and patients with down syndrome, in addition to teaching adults to read and write, and serving breakfast to the less fortunate every morning.

Born in 1943 in the City of Sanandaj of Kurdistan province, **Mohammad Assad Seraj-aldini** had an especial interest in radio broadcasting from the very beginning. An interest that gravitated him toward the capital city in 1963 to start a career—first in Tehran and later in Kermanshah—as a broadcaster, anchorperson, and Kurdish translator at the National Radio of Iran, during which time he collaborated with another well-respected anchorperson, his wife Parvin Moshir-vazir. The couple's programs reached beyond the borders of Iran, and were heard within the Kurdish communities of Iraq and Syria as well. Their outstanding programs in Kurdish—written and produced by Seraj-aldini—was much respected and supported by the Royal government of Iran. At the time of the 1979 revolution, Seraj-aldini was the senior director of the Kurdish programs at Radio Sanandaj, but after the revolution, the Seraj-aldini family found living in Iran unbearable, and left the country through Zagros mountain range. The family first settled in Kurdistan of Iraq and later in England. Mohammad Assad Seraj-aldini has published many articles in Persian and Kurdish, has collected and edited five volumes of poetry by A'abed Seraj-aldini, and has been working on a collection of poetry in Persian and Kurdish by the Sufi patriarch Sheikh Mowlana Naghshbandi.

Author

Shirindokht Nourmanesh is a creative writer, a fine artist, a literary translator and an independent researcher—with a focus on symbolism in writings of Iranian women. A published author with two compilations of short stories and several fiction and non-fiction pieces, she is the Iranian editor for *The Third Script*, stories from Iran, Tasmania, & the UK.

Shirindokht is the founder of *Vesta Arts & Lectures*, co-founder of the San Jose City College *Middle Eastern Heritage Month*, the co-founder of *Red Chair Writing Workshop*, and the co-founder of Gerdayesh for the academic study of Shahnameh. She was the last director of the Association of Iranian American Writers and one of the three jurists for the *No to Censorship Contest* by Siamak Pourzand Foundation.

A former lecturer at San Jose State University, Shirindokht now works as the development manager at Pars Equality Center, and pursues a Ph.D. in transpersonal psychology.

www.ingramcontent.com/pod-product-compliance
Lightning Source LLC
Chambersburg PA
CBHW071952100426
42736CB00043B/3066